Hillrocks Coloring Book

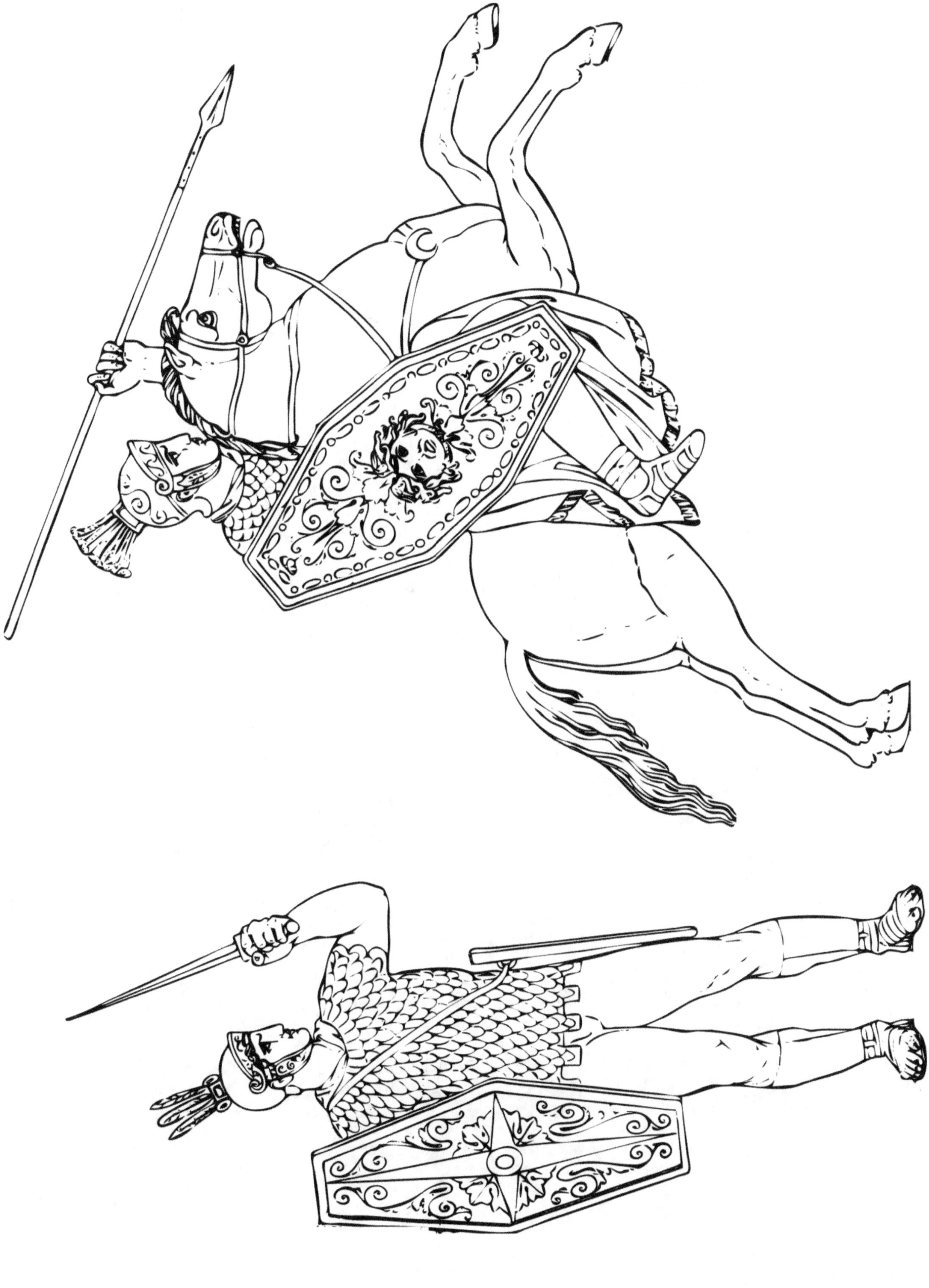

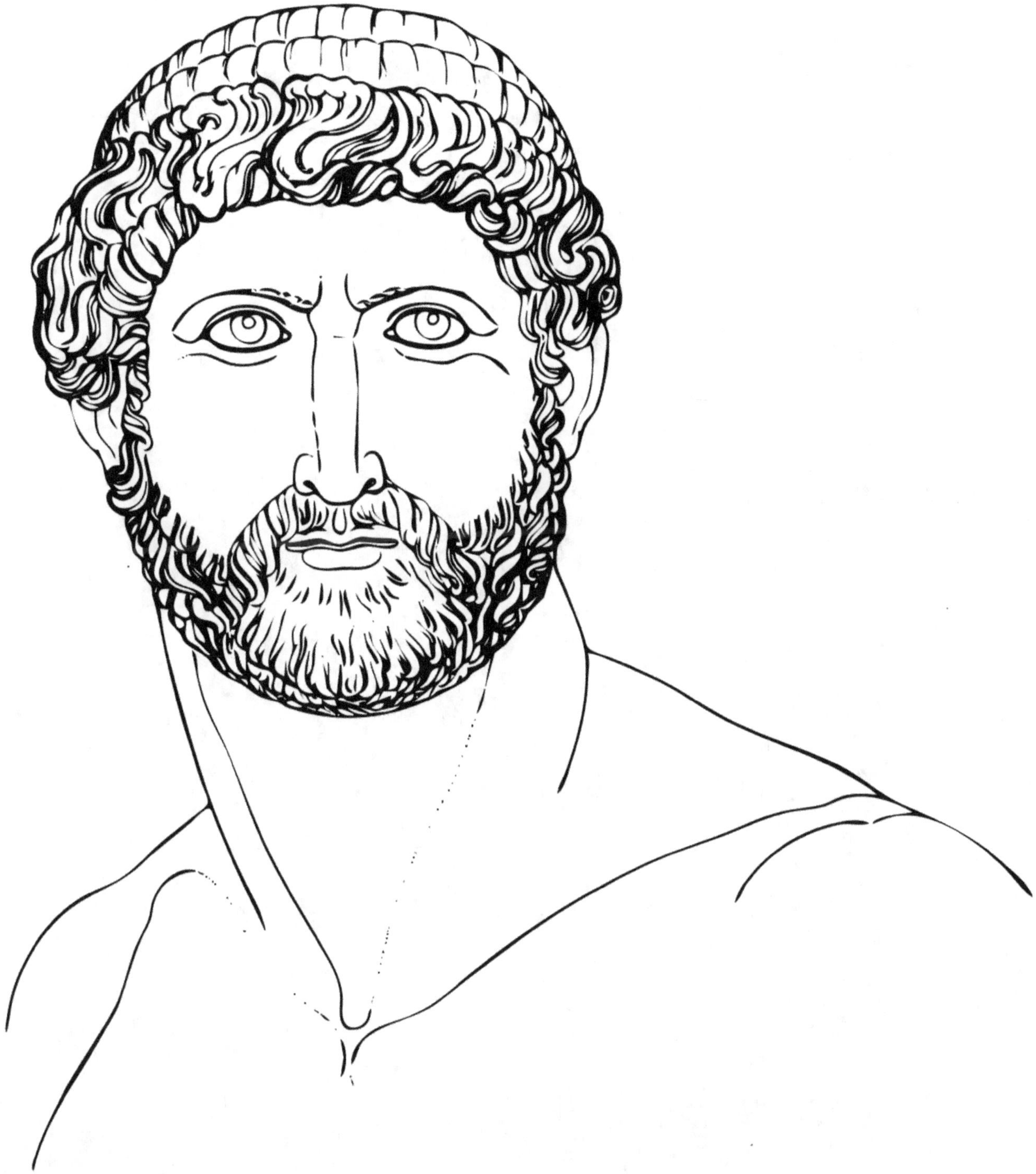

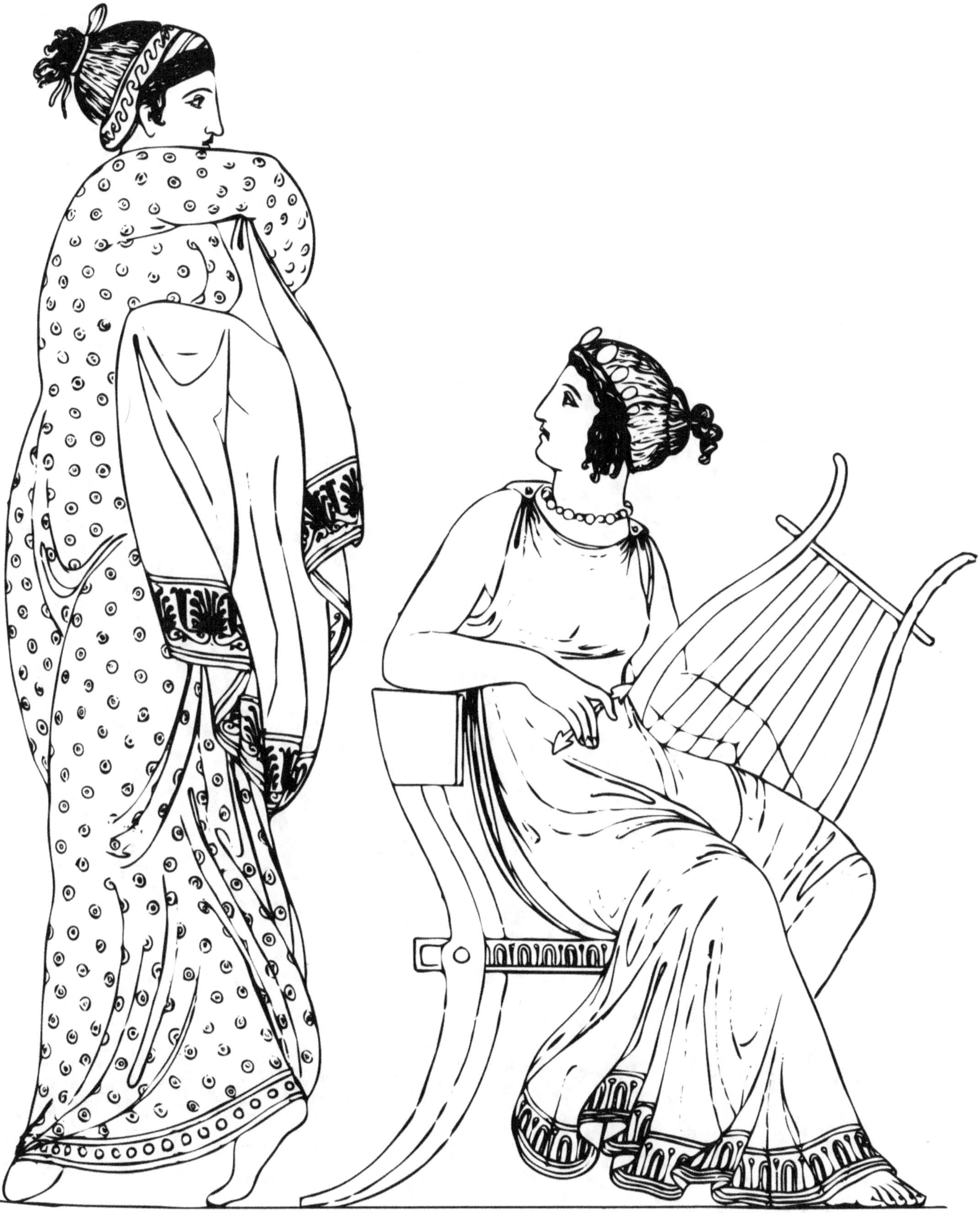

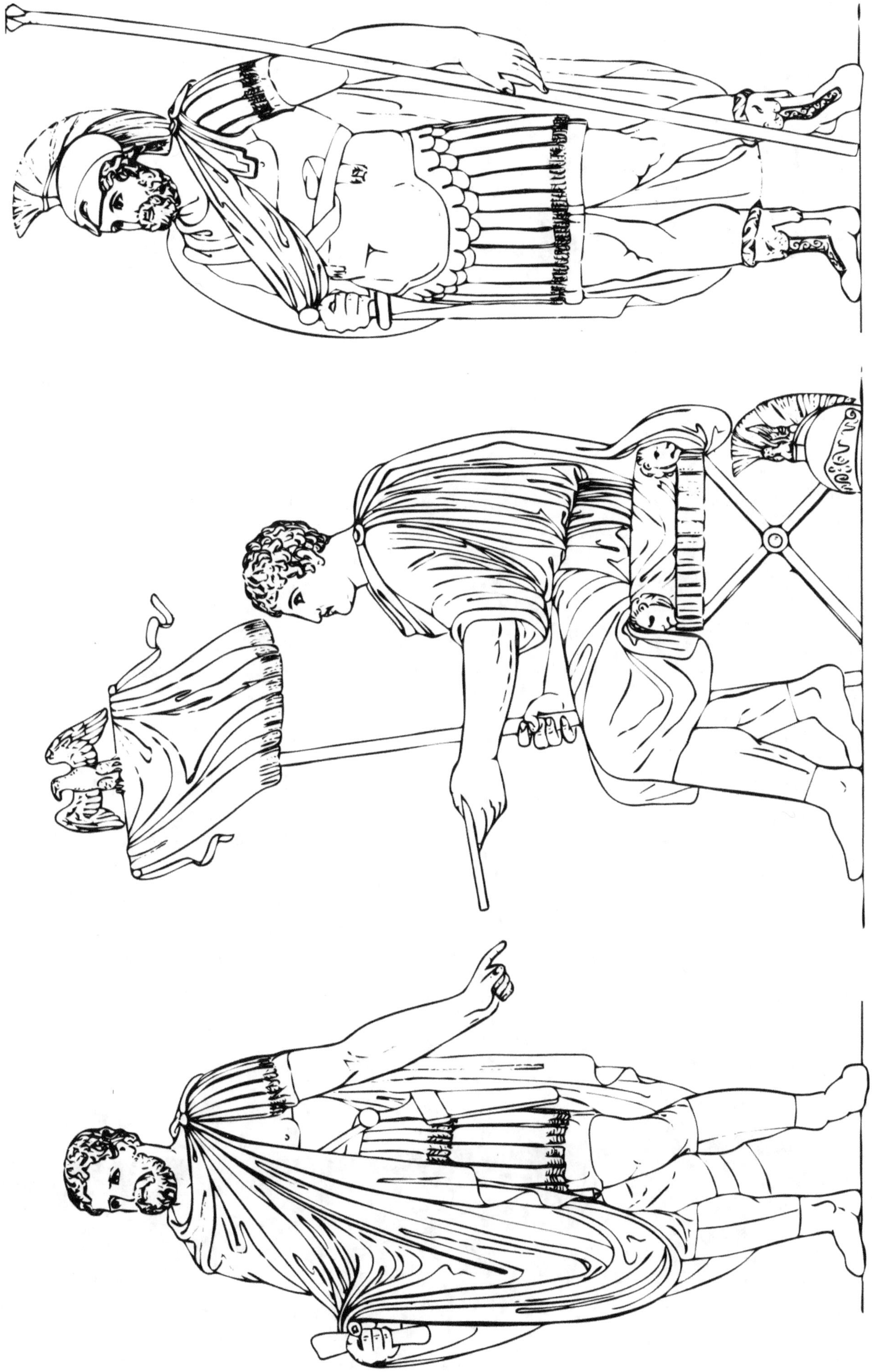

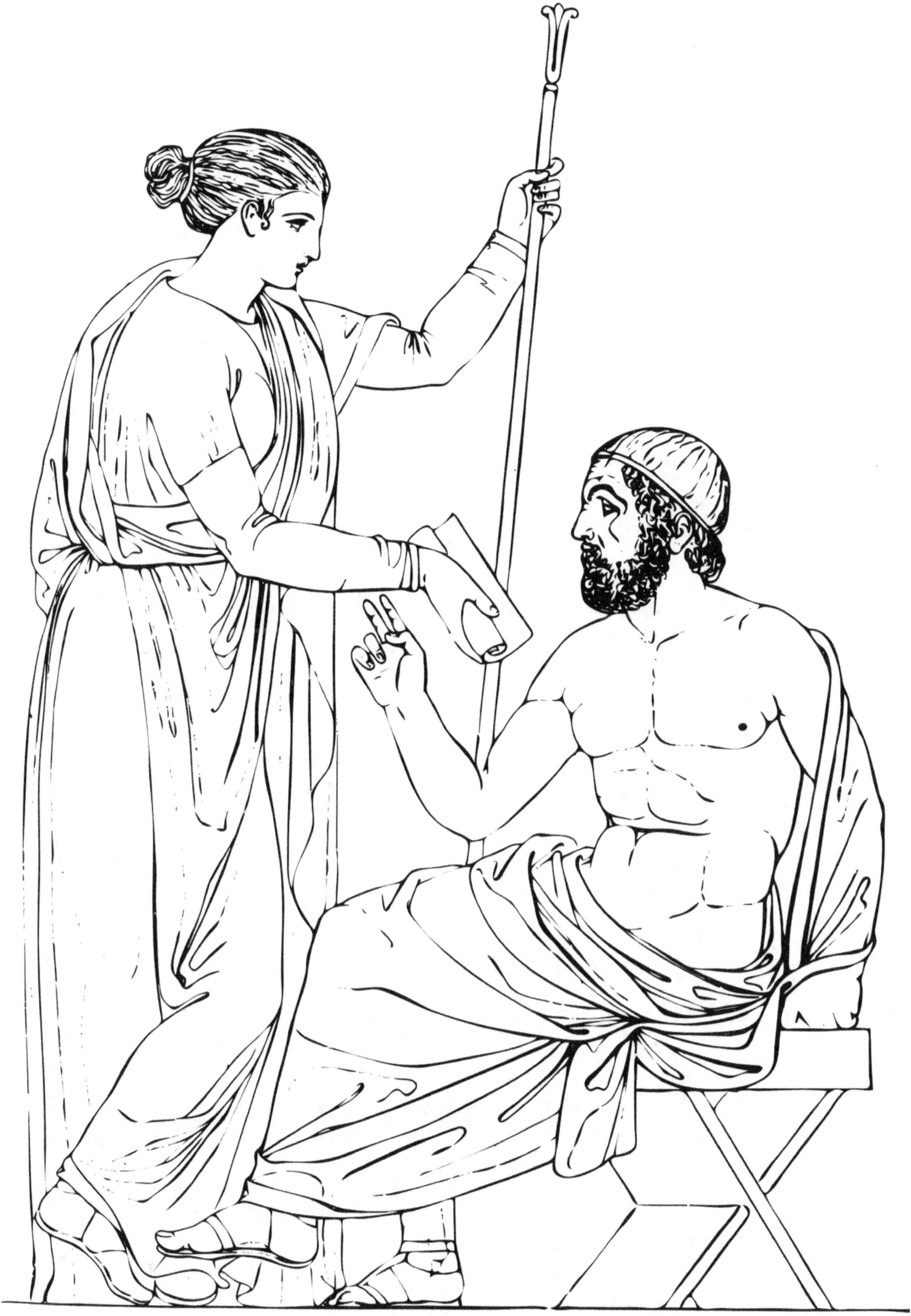

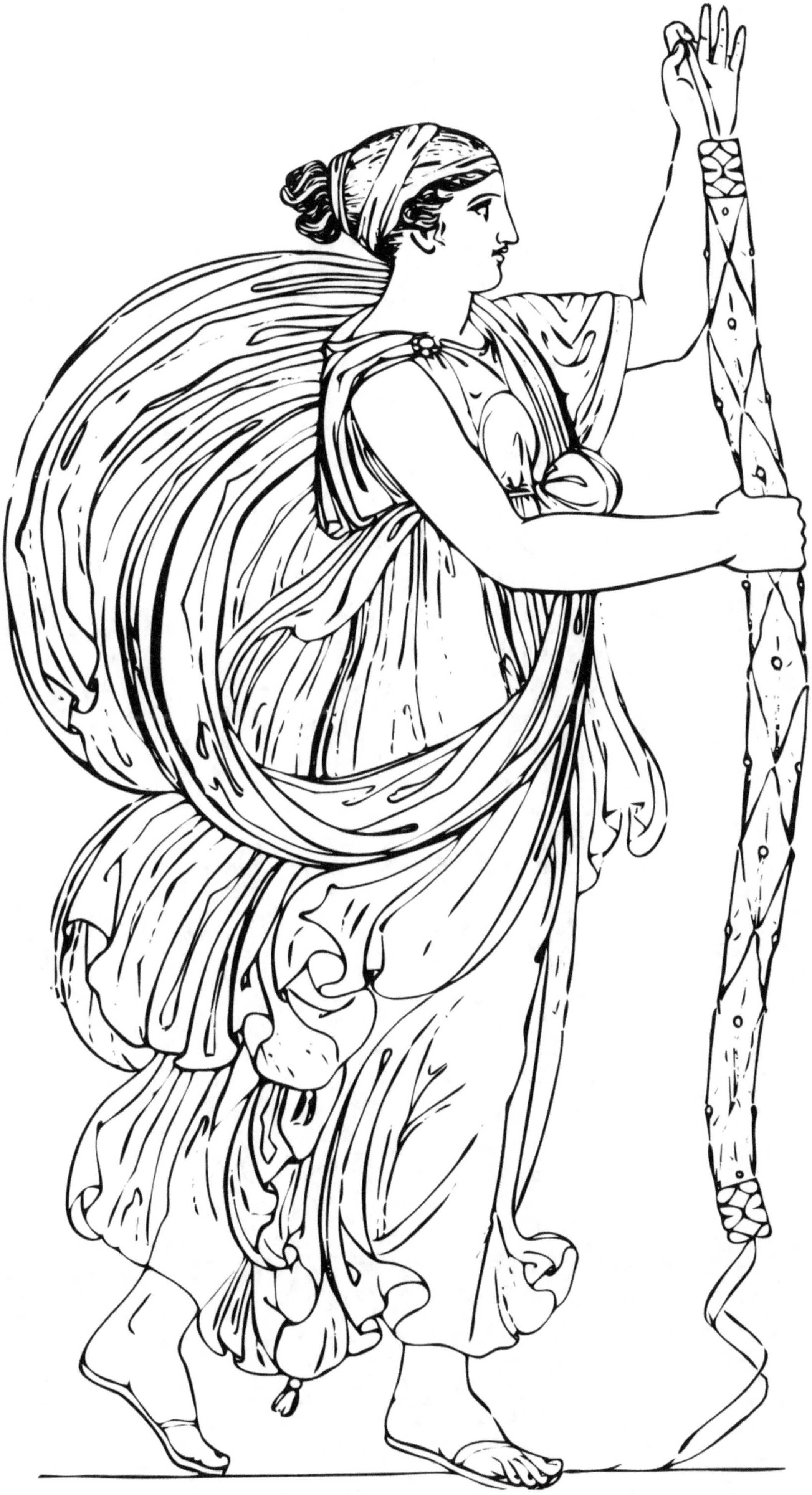

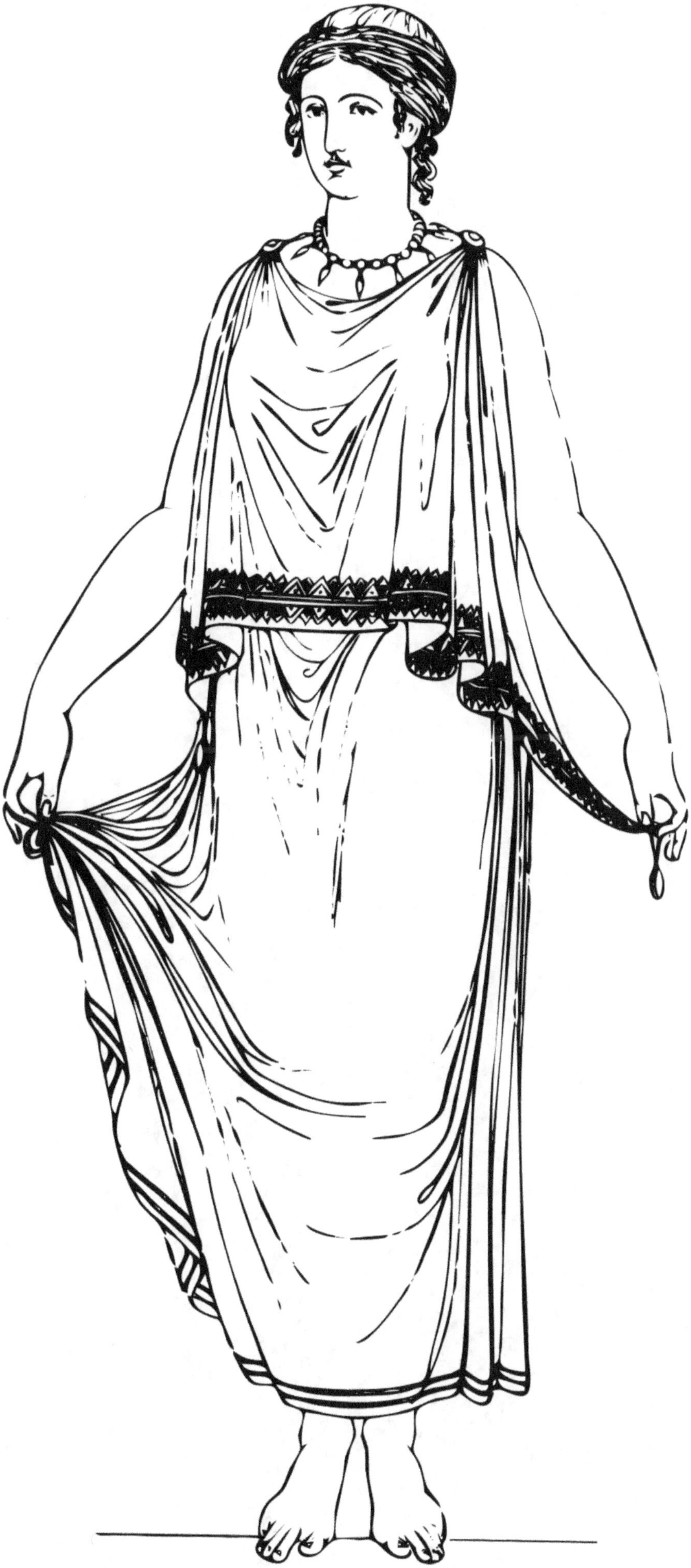

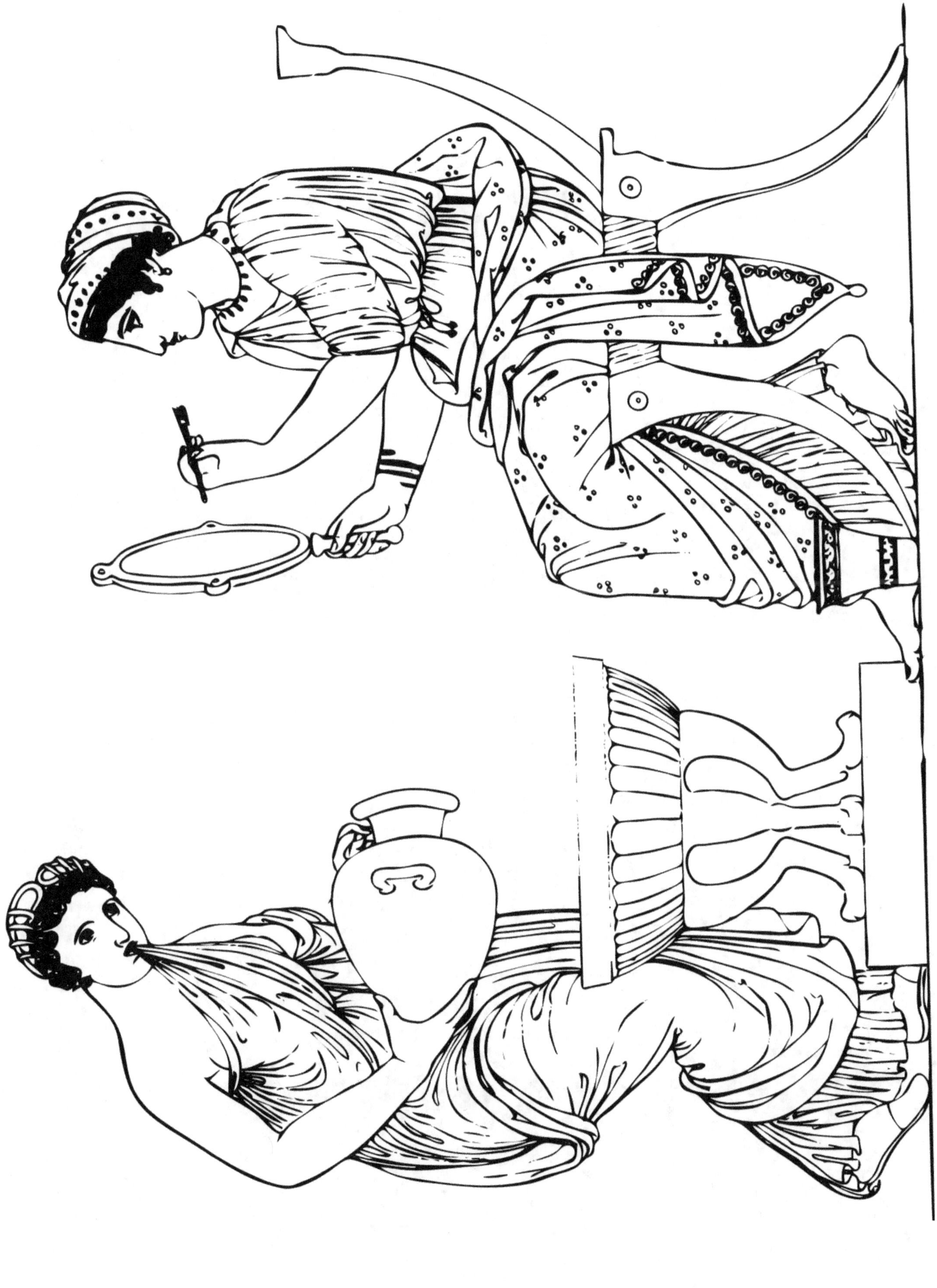

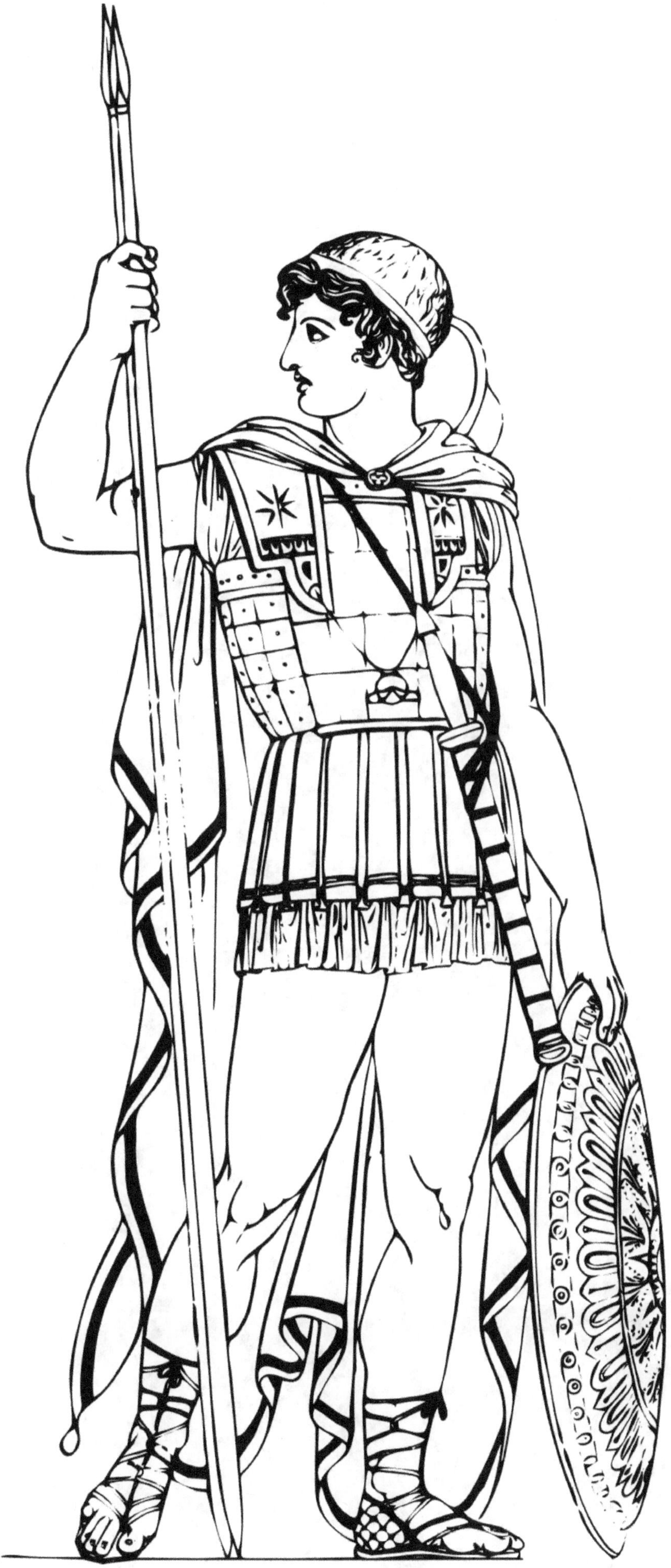

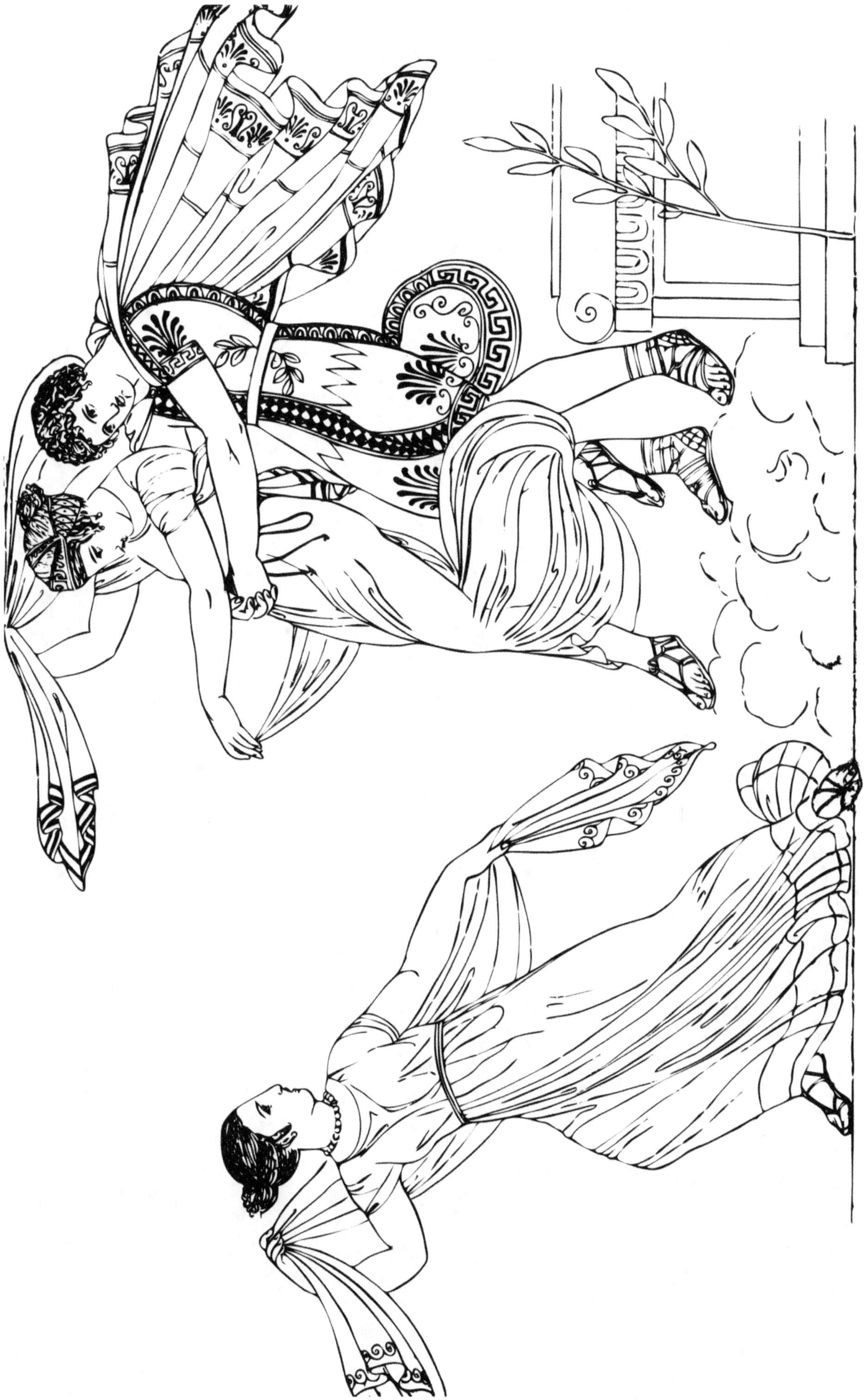

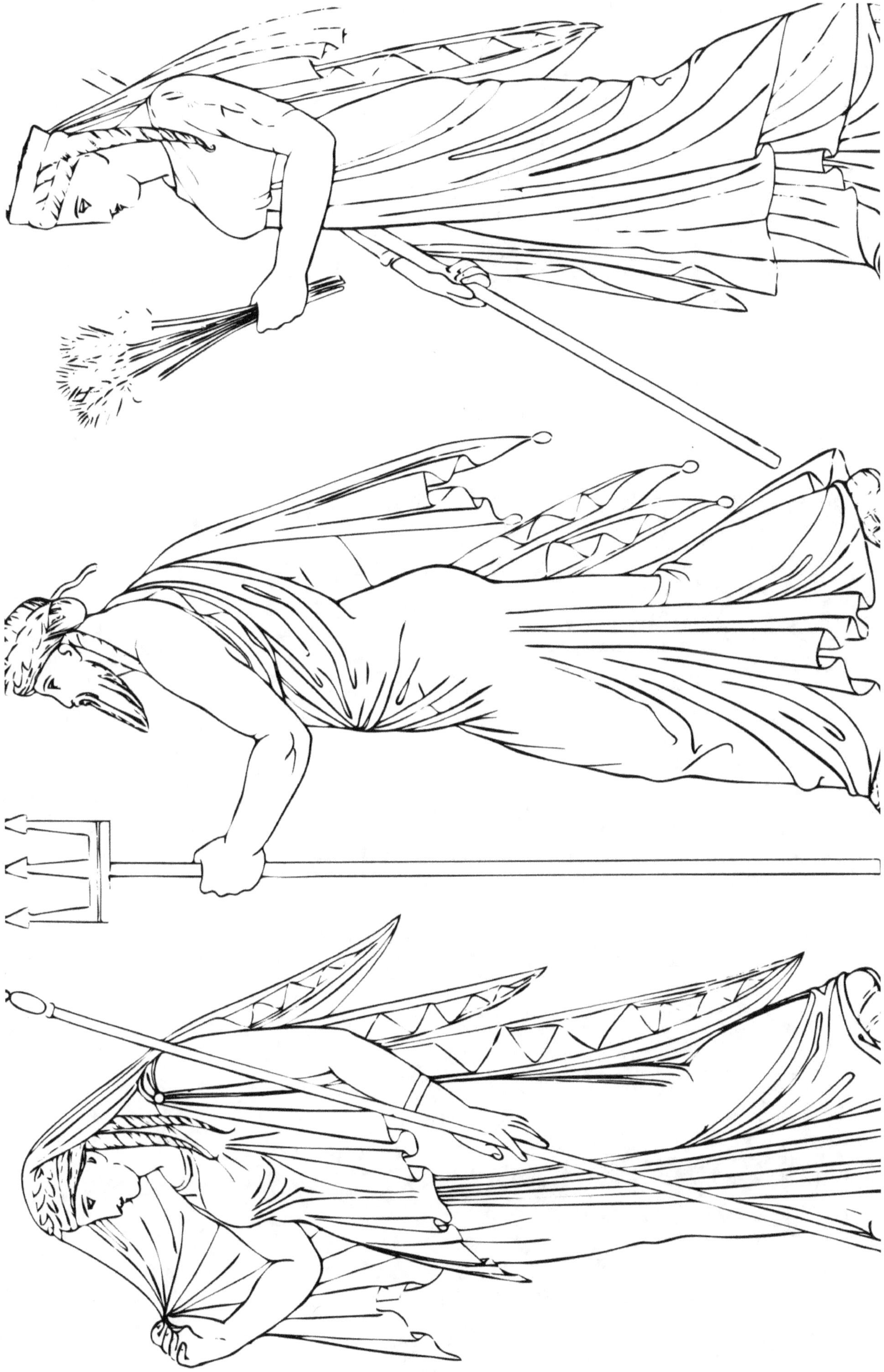

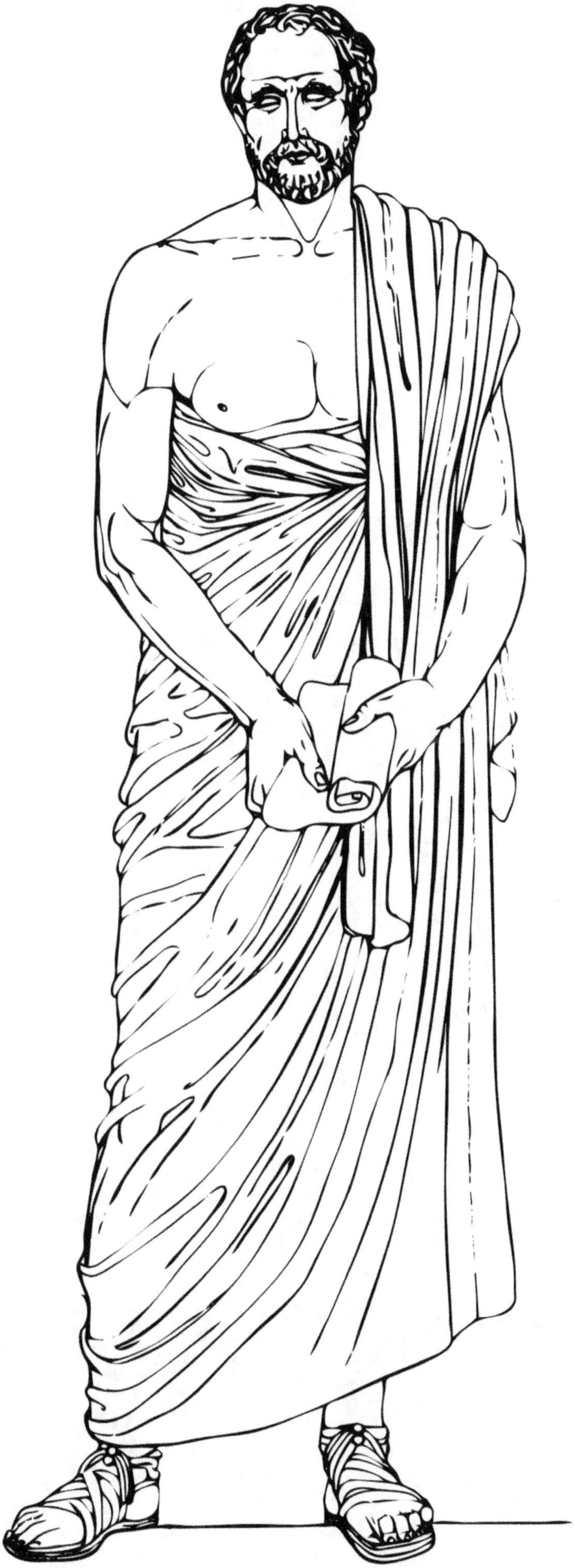

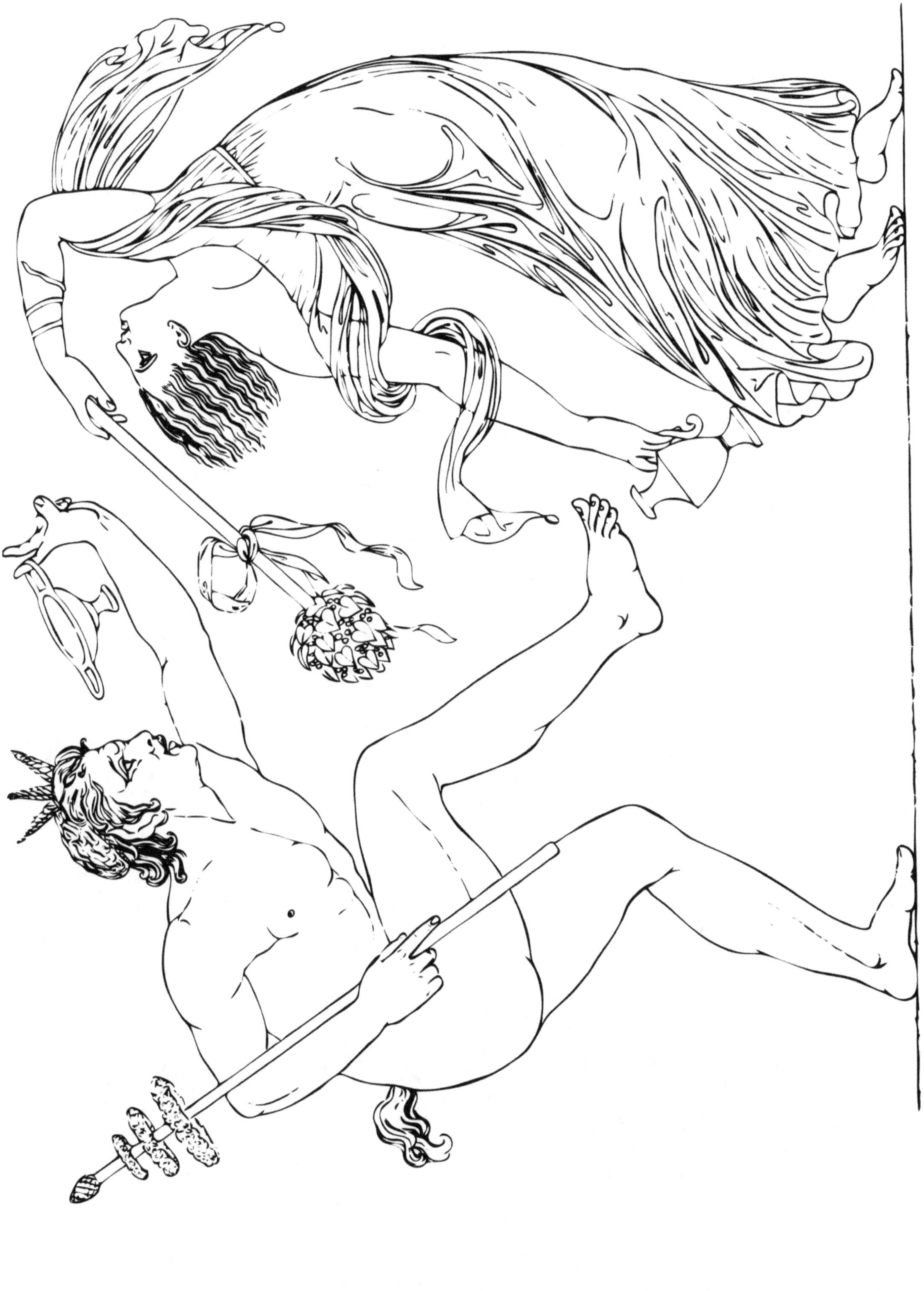

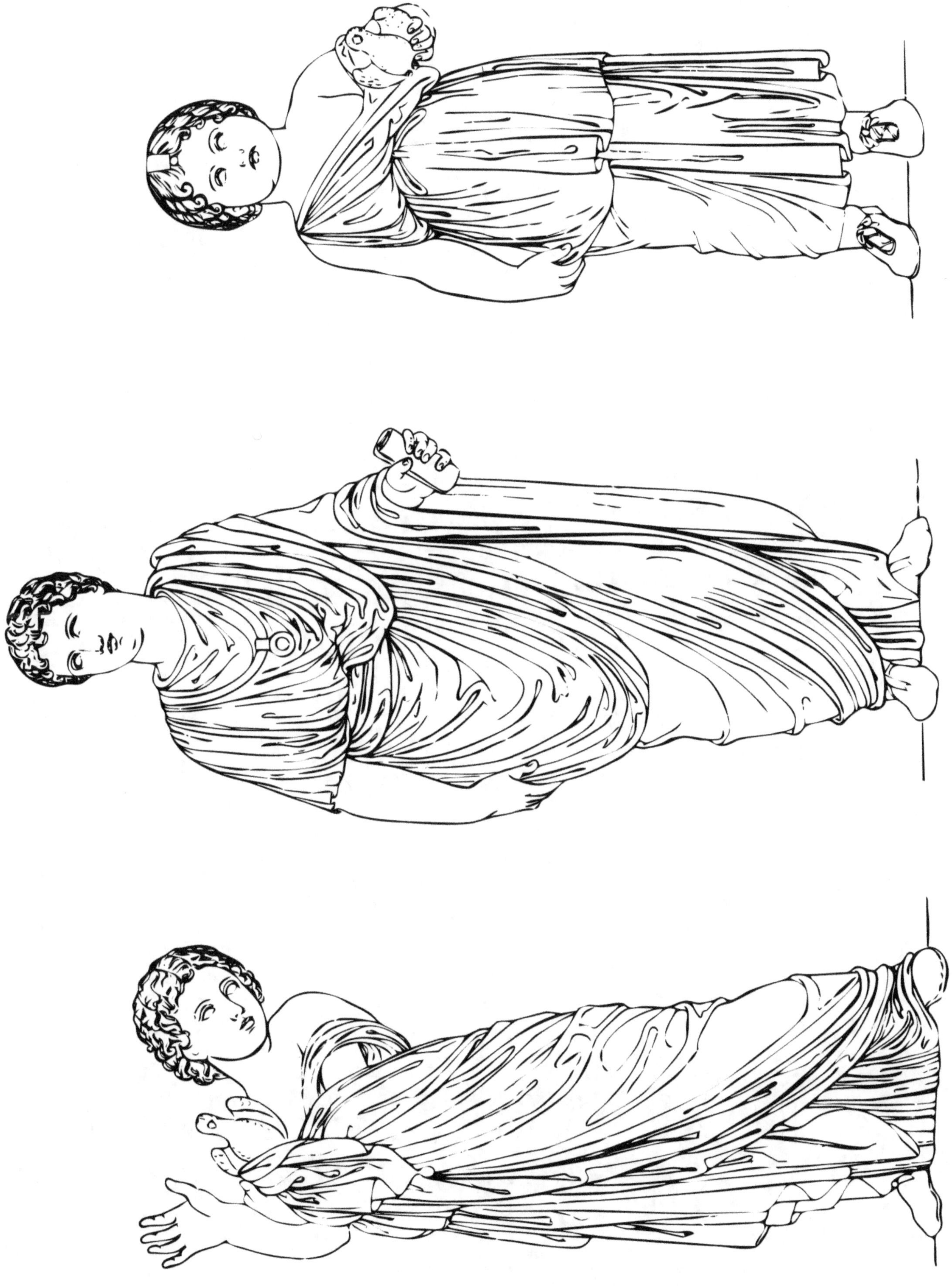

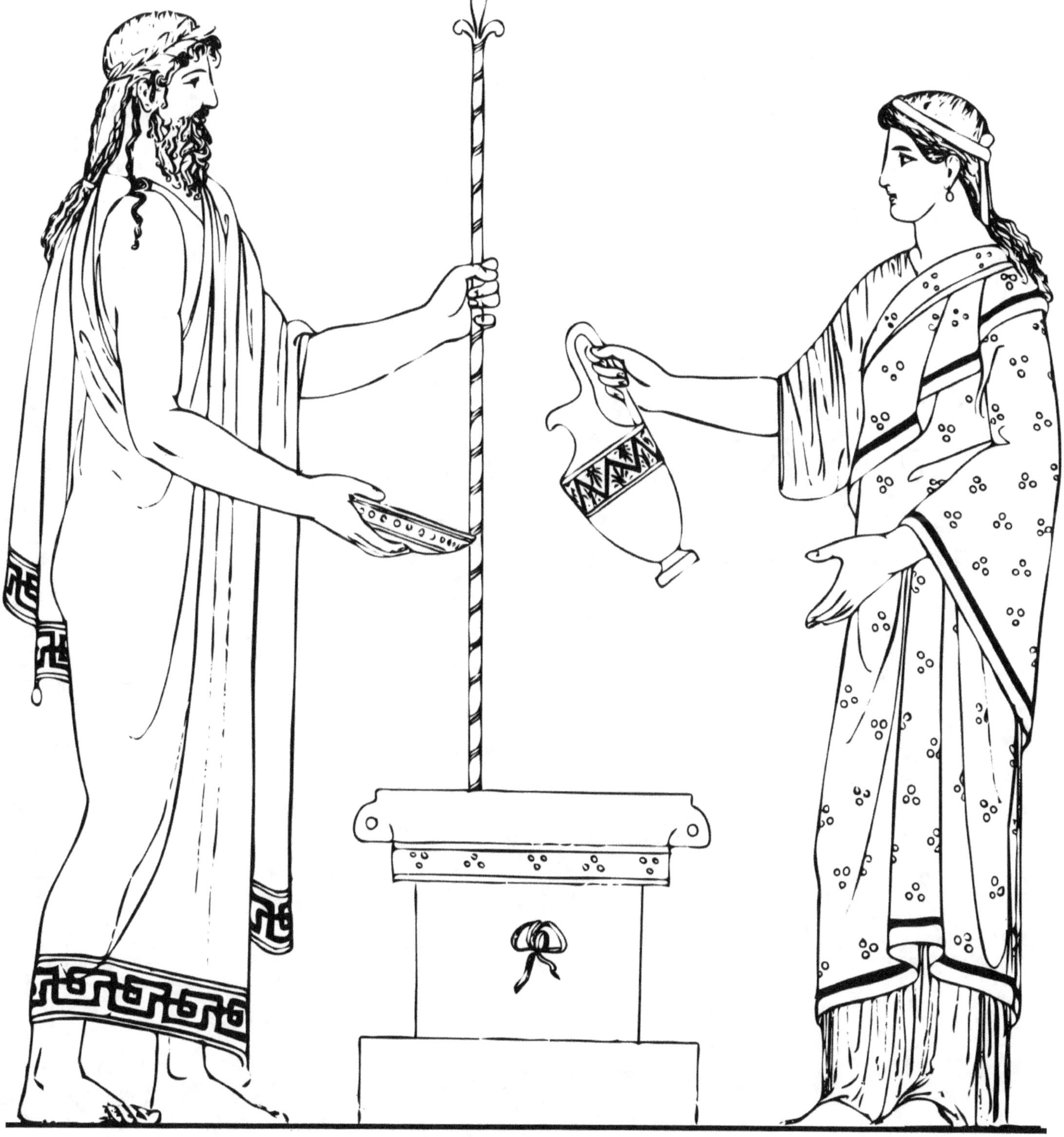

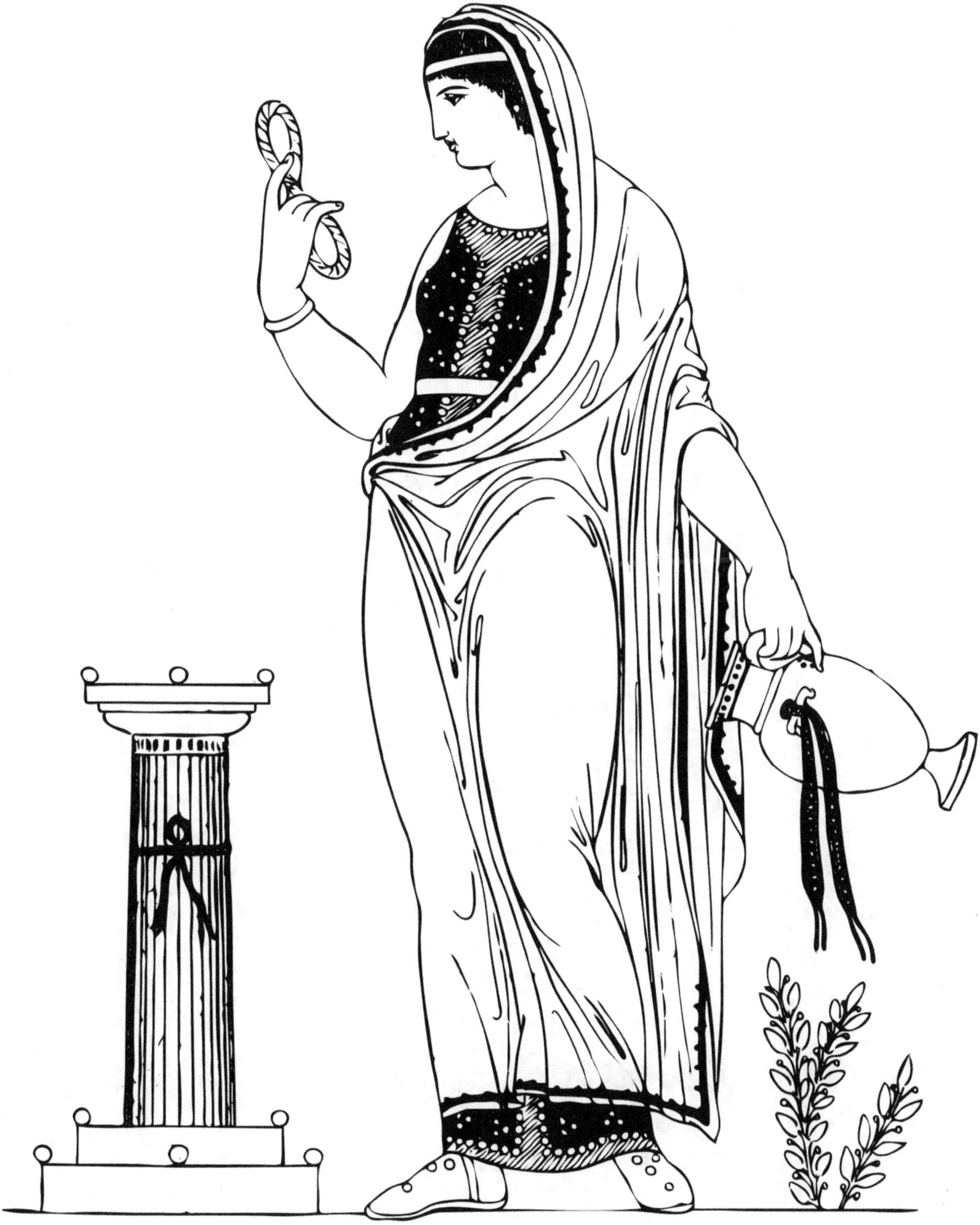

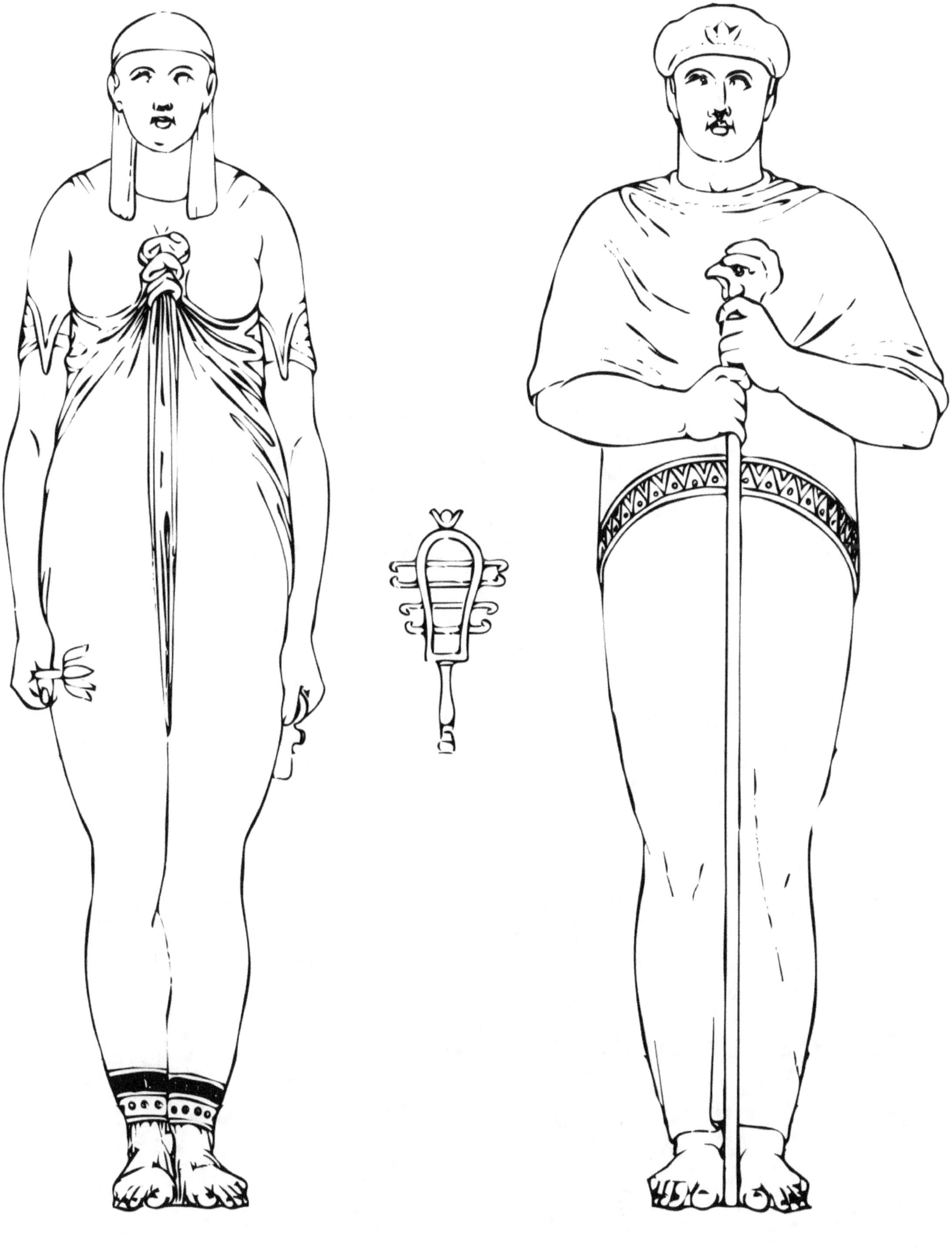

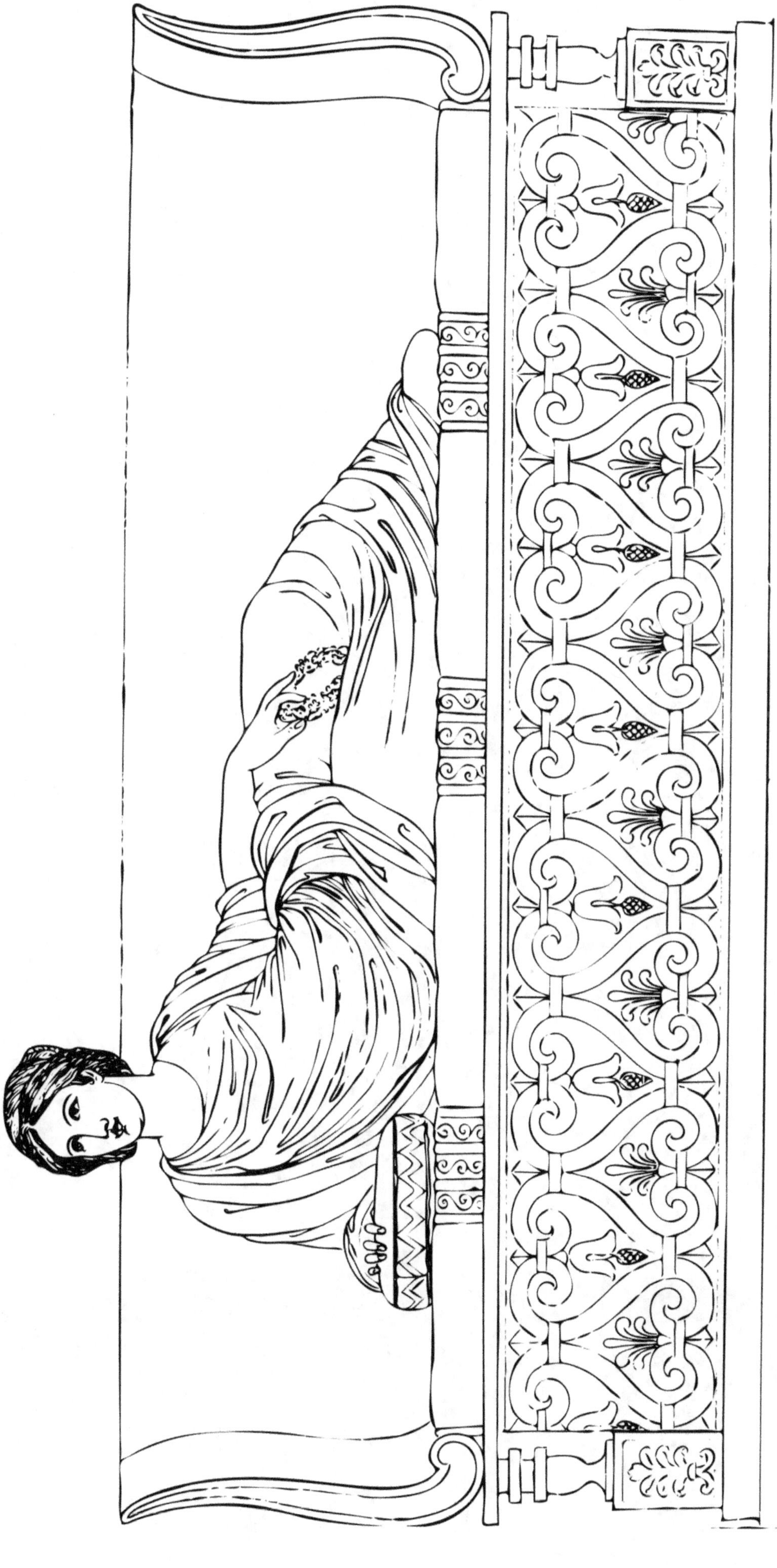

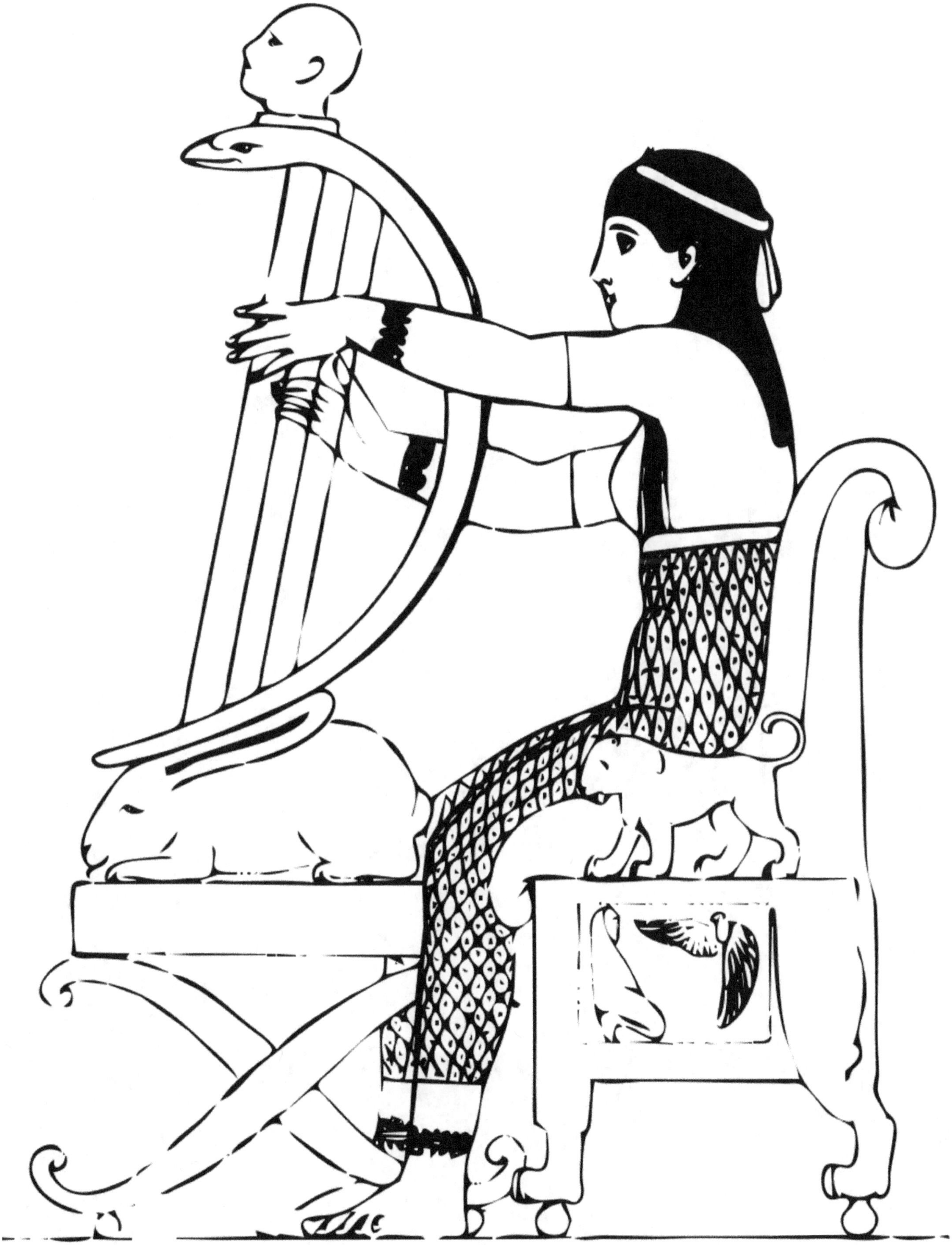

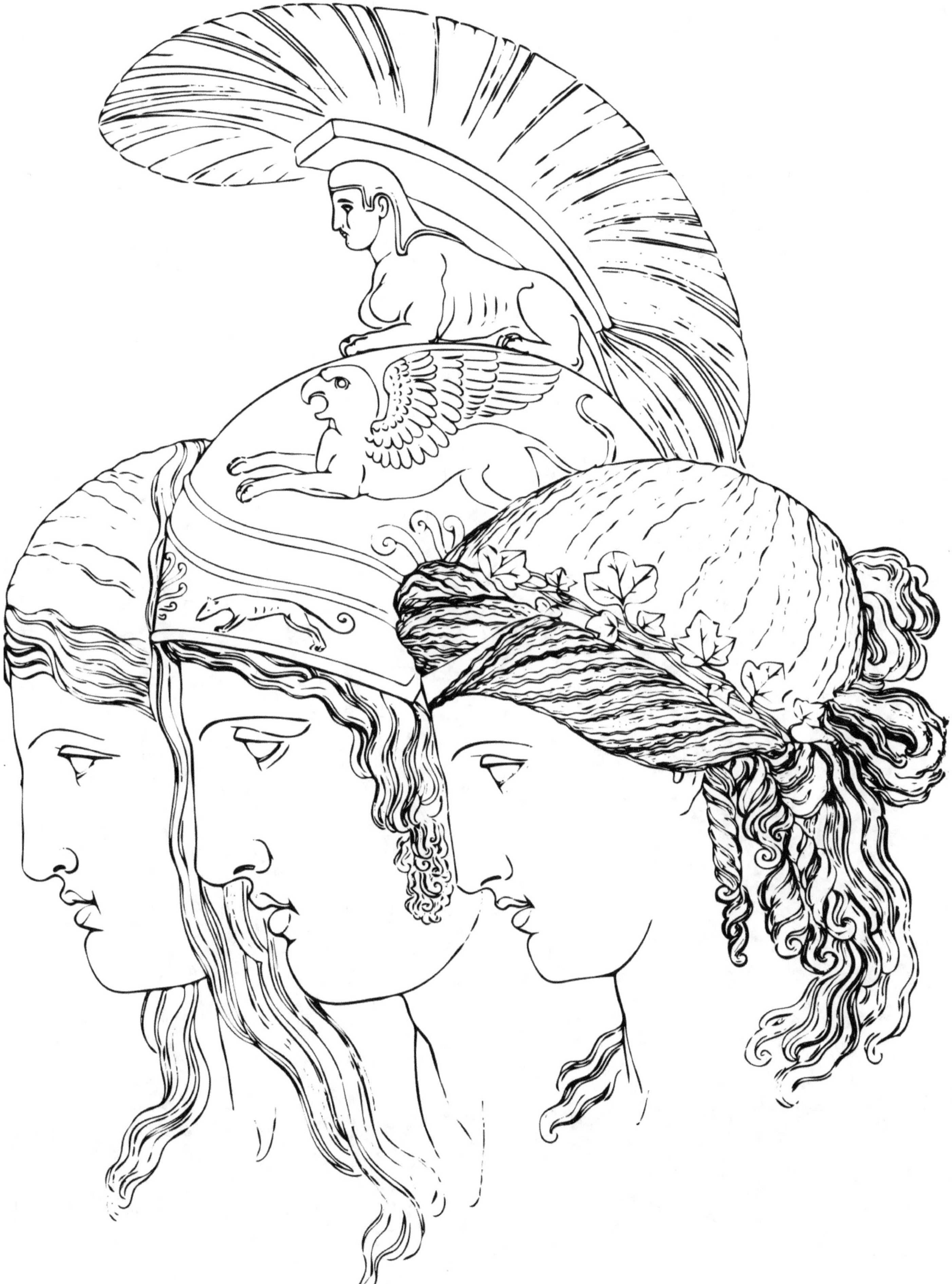

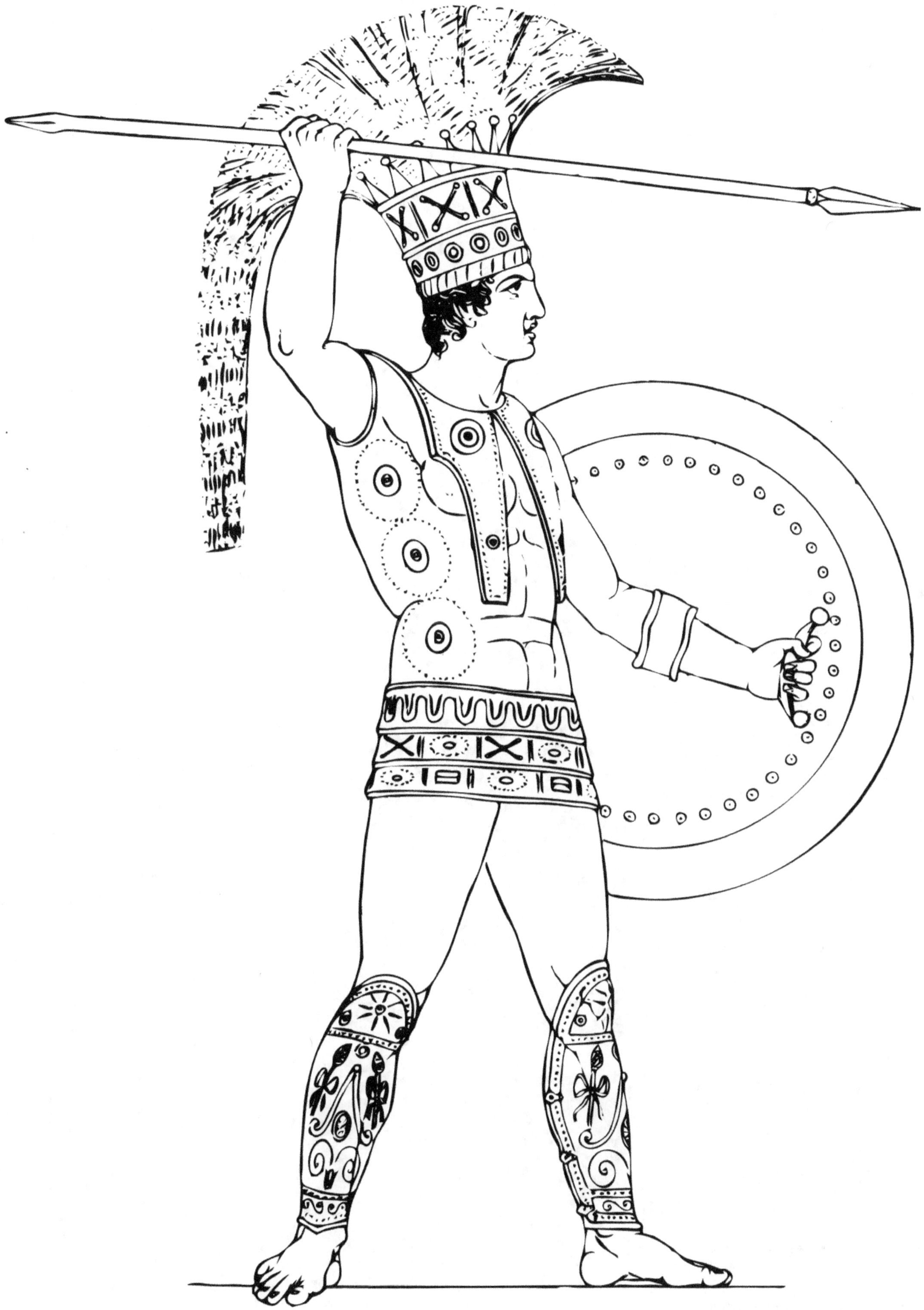

www.ingramcontent.com/pod-product-compliance
Lightning Source LLC
Chambersburg PA
CBHW081420220526
45467CB00009B/2752
9781708371081